Mobi
COMMO

MW00681847

Mobil New Zealand Nature Series
COMMON BIRDS IN NEW ZEALAND 1

TOWN, PASTURE AND FRESHWATER BIRDS

**Janet Marshall
F. C. Kinsky
C. J. R. Robertson**

HEINEMANN REED

Published by Heinemann Reed, a division of Octopus
Publishing Group (NZ) Ltd, 39 Rawene Road, Birkenhead,
Auckland. Associated companies, branches and
representatives throughout the world.

ISBN 0 7900 0159 4

© 1975, Janet Marshall (paintings)
       F. C. Kinsky and C. J. R. Robertson (text)
First published 1975
Reprinted 1977, 1980, 1985, 1989, 1990

Printed in Singapore

Contents

Foreword

Nobody can say for certain whether there are more
birds than people in New Zealand, or *vice versa,* but
that is an academic question compared with the
certainty that while the number of people in the country
is increasing, the number of wild birds, on land anyway,
is declining. This trend can only be arrested as we
show more concern for the welfare of birds, and
awareness of their basic need for a healthy
environment. Ironically, we are slow to realise that this
is a basic need for ourselves as well as for the birds.

Most of us get to know a few birds by direct
observation, but when unfamiliar ones begin to pose a
challenge we tend to give up. The alternative is to look
for a bird book, and that brings the problem of what
kind to choose. There is now a considerable range
of choice available from scientific treatise to tailored
field guide. You may be an enthusiast and need the lot,
but more probably your immediate requirement is
something handy for recognition, with an emphasis on
the species most commonly seen.

This, it seems to me, is that kind of book; and if the
writer of a foreword can venture an opinion about its
contents, I should like to commend the breakaway from
emphasis on the species usually regarded as native,
and the equality of treatment accorded to those
generally labelled "introduced", whether they became
established a hundred years ago, or just last year.
Some visiting botanists recently commented on the
numbing effect on our understanding of the vegetation
of a preoccupation with native plant studies, and it is
just as true in the realm of animal life. The impact and

contribution of the house-sparrow in the whole pattern of wildlife is just as significant as that of the fantail. Biologists, of course, recognise this as a fact of ecology, but it is taking a long time to filter down to the level of popular understanding. The readers of this book may be assured that every one of the birds figured and described has something to contribute to their enlightenment and enjoyment.

R. A. Falla, CMG, MA, DSc, FRSNZ

Introduction

Few people should be unaware of the birds inhabiting our environment. Some birds are more obvious because of their number or habits, while others may be plentiful but more secretive. Many of the most commonly seen birds have been introduced by man since 1850. Some of these have replaced those native and endemic birds which have failed to survive man's modification of the environment and introduced animals such as cats and rats. Some birds, both native and introduced, are considered pests because they compete with man for the produce of crops, orchards and even the family vegetable garden which provide an abundant and varied food store. The resulting losses are invariably followed by demands for control and even extermination. Unfortunately, the end result is often the destruction of species other than the ones we are trying to destroy. However, many birds, including those often considered troublesome, perform a useful function in naturally controlling other animal pests without the cost of chemicals and the increasing side effects of pollution. Further, the increasingly rapid modification of the land for towns, industry and agriculture has resulted in the loss of valuable forest and wetland habitat which has seriously affected many species.

There has been an increasing number of books devoted to New Zealand birds in recent years. However, there has been a tendency to write about, photograph and paint only the native or endemic species and ignore the numerous introduced birds which have become an integral part of the New

Zealand bird fauna. The major authoritative reference works on the other hand are probably too detailed for any person not having a specific interest in birds, and in addition these works generally lack a complete coverage of illustrations.

This volume, the first of two on the common or commonly-seen birds of New Zealand, is not designed as a field guide or as a text book, but for use in practical visual identification. The object has been through colour portraits of each species to give a visual image, complemented by a brief summary of information designed more as an incentive for further interest and study, rather than an exhaustive reference.

The species chosen for Volume One covering *Town, Pasture and Freshwater* are not the only birds seen in these habitats, nor are these the only areas in which they are found. However, some arbitrary decisions were required and most of the introduced birds were confined to this volume, reflecting their continuing close association with man. Volume Two covering Mountain, Bush and Shore habitats records predominantly native and endemic species prominent in those parts of the country least directly modified by man. Volume Three covers the uncommon birds of New Zealand.

With the growing interest and demand for conservation of our environment, one of the major handicaps is a lack of precise information. There is often too great a reliance on sentiment and opinion unsupported by facts. Birds are not only nice to look at, but because they are readily seen they may also be a major indicator of changes in our environment. The sudden appearance of large numbers of dead birds makes a greater impact on people than the same number of insects. An interest in what has happened is the first step toward the action required for possible prevention in the future. We hope that both at home and while travelling this book will stimulate your interest and improve your understanding. All birds have their place and importance; let us conserve and enjoy what we have, regardless of sentiment and without differentiation.

Notes on Text

The birds appear in the same order as in the **Annotated Checklist of the Birds of New Zealand** except where two species are shown on one plate. Common, scientific and where available Maori names are shown according to the **Checklist.**

Species are divided into three categories.

Endemic — confined solely to the New Zealand region.

Native — naturally occurring in New Zealand, but also found elsewhere in the world.

Introduced — introduced by human agency.

Scientific names are the only certain way of referring to any bird, as common names so often vary throughout the country and may be shared by several species.

Though we have tried to use simple language for all descriptions an occasional specific term such as "speculum" (conspicuously coloured area on duck's wings) has been used.

♂ – Male   ♀ – Female

DABCHICK

Summer

Winter

New Zealand Dabchick

Podiceps rufopectus

(Weweia)

Family: PODICIPEDIDAE

Endemic: (Fully protected)

Field Characters:
- half size of Grey Duck.
- small head, short pointed bill.
- throat and upper chest reddish-brown.
- underparts white with brown mottling on flanks.
- no tail, rump high when swimming.
- rapid head-first dive.
- Immature: cheeks grey, throat and upper chest pale reddish-brown, under-parts white.

Distribution and Habitat:
- North Island lakes, ponds, and coastal lagoons, rare in South Island.
- not generally on rivers.
- feeds in shallow fresh water on insects and snails.

Breeding:
- August to May.
- Nest: flimsy but bulky structure floating among and attached to water-edge vegetation.
- Eggs: 2-3, chalky-white quickly stained yellowish-brown, covered with weed when unattended.
- small chicks with striped plumage may be carried on the backs of swimming parents.

PLATE 1

13

WHITE – FACED HERON

White-faced Heron

Ardea novaehollandiae

Family: ARDEIDAE

Native: Self-introduced from Australia, rare till 1940s. (Fully protected)

Field Characters:
- white face, light blue-grey body.
- dark grey wing feathers contrasting in flight with paler body.
- neck retracted in flight.
- slow, leisurely wing beat.
- Immature: generally similar to adult, but with indistinct white face.

Distribution and Habitat:
- most common heron, widespread throughout New Zealand.
- all habitats except bush, rarely alpine, usually seashore, ponds, lakes, rivers, and open pasture.
- often perches on trees and fence posts.
- may be seen in large groups.
- feeds mainly on land and water insects (dragonflies, grasshoppers, blowflies, etc.), also fish, frogs and small mammals.

Breeding:
- August to December.
- Nest: small, untidy, flimsy, of sticks, found singly in high trees. (Not colonial)
- Eggs: 3-5, light blue with white chalky marks.

PLATE 2

15

BITTERN

Bittern

(Matuku)

Botaurus stellaris

Family: ARDEIDAE

Native: Also found Australia and New Caledonia.
   (Fully protected)

Field Characters:
   - bulkier than White-faced Heron with shorter legs, and neck appearing stout and shorter.
   - all buff-brown with dark streaking.
   - in flight, slow wing beat, with neck tucked in.
   - if disturbed in cover often "freezes" with head and bill erect.
   - very secretive.
   - Voice: loud booming at night.

Distribution and Habitat:
   - throughout New Zealand, rarely seen in open.
   - swamps, lakes, salt marshes and boggy areas with cover.
   - feeds on wide variety of food, mainly insects, fish and eels, frogs and small mammals.

Breeding:
   - September to January.
   - Nest: large firm platform of rushes, reeds and sticks, usually surrounded by water and well hidden in reed beds and between clumps of niggerheads.
   - Eggs: 4-5, plain brownish-cream, without spots.

PLATE 3

17

BLACK SWAN

Black Swan

Cygnus atratus

Family: ANATIDAE

Introduced: From Australia prior to 1864 and during 1860s in both islands. (Protected but may be hunted in open season)

Field Characters:
- very large, predominantly black.
- white wing feathers conspicuous in flight.
- bill mainly ruby-red.
- outstretched neck in flight, ponderous wing beat.
- Immature: grey, with dark bill.

Distribution and Habitat:
- throughout New Zealand on medium to large lakes and lagoons.
- mainly coastal, rare in some districts, but large breeding populations, especially at Lake Ellesmere and the Waikato lakes.
- feeds on water plants in shallow water to greater depth than ducks.

Breeding:
- Mainly August to November.
- Nest: substantial mound of grass and rushes lined with down and close to water, normally single surrounded by tall vegetation. By some large lakes (e.g., Lake Ellesmere) colonial breeding on open ground.
- Eggs: 4-7, greenish-white.

Mute Swan

Cygnus olor

NOTE:
A rare, larger, pure white swan, with orange bill and prominent black knob at base of bill, may be seen occasionally associated with flocks of Black Swan in the wild (fully protected). Introduced originally for ornamental purposes and still seen in public parks.

PLATE 4

19

CANADA GOOSE

Canada Goose

Branta canadensis
Family: ANATIDAE

Introduced: From North America 1876-1905. (Not protected, except in certain areas)

Field Characters:
- somewhat smaller than Black Swan, with shorter neck.
- colour buff, with black neck and white cheeks.
- in flight, outstretched neck, fast wingbeat.
- Immature: black parts are dark brown.

Distribution and Habitat:
- South Island, east of main divide, rare in North Island.
- high country and larger lakes where they may concentrate in large moulting flocks during late summer.
- feeds on grass and green fodder crops.

Breeding:
- October to December.
- Nest: on ground, of grasses and tussock lined with down, generally in high country.
- Eggs: 4-7, creamy-white.
- Female only incubates, male usually on guard nearby.

PLATE 5

21

PARADISE DUCK

Paradise Duck
(Putangitangi)

Tadorna variegata
Family: ANATIDAE

Endemic: (Protected but may be hunted in open season in some localities)

Field Characters:
- size between Mallard and Canada Goose.
- Male: predominantly black with metallic sheen on head.
- Female: white head, dark back, rusty brown undersides.
- in flight, both sexes show prominent large white patch on wing.
- Immature: similar to adult male.

Distribution and Habitat:
- throughout both islands reaching high density in some areas, generally increasing where protected.
- open hill country, riverbeds, small lakes and ponds, and open pasture.
- large moulting flocks on some lakes in late summer.
- feeds on soft grasses and herbs, some insects.

Breeding:
- August to January.
- Nest: of grass and down, generally well hidden on ground, sometimes in hollow trees up to 20ft.
- not necessarily adjacent to water.
- Eggs: 5-11, cream.
- female only incubates, but male assists in rearing young.

PLATE 6   23

MALLARD DUCK

♀

♂

Mallard

Anas platyrynchos
Family: ANATIDAE

Introduced: From Britain since 1867 and later also from USA. Extensive liberations from hand-reared stock till 1950s. (Protected but may be hunted in open season)

Field Characters:
- Male: two plumages, "breeding plumage" very conspicuous as in plate.
- "Eclipse plumage" (late summer and autumn) similar to female, but male recognisable by **olive-green** bill.
- Female: may be confused with Grey Duck, but is a browner bird generally lacking striped face.
- orange feet, bill **dark olive-brown** with individually variable orange mottling.
- speculum shiny blue, with white stripe at both margins.
- pale sides to tail showing in flight.
- Immature: like female.

Distribution and Habitat:
- throughout New Zealand.
- rapidly increasing in proportion to Grey Duck, especially in south.
- habitat and feeding as for Grey Duck.

Breeding:
- August to December.
- Nest: similar to Grey Duck but often close to water or margins of wetlands in any available cover (e.g., niggerheads and in raupo).
- Eggs: 5-20, cream with light green tinge.
- female only incubates and cares for young.

Note:
Extensive interbreeding with ducks of similar size (including domestic) has produced widely mixed hybrid plumages.

PLATE 7

25

GREY DUCK

Grey Duck

(Parera)

Anas superciliosa

Family: ANATIDAE

Native: Also Australia. (Protected but may be hunted in open
season)

Field Characters:
- somewhat smaller than Mallard.
- male and female indistinguishable.
- conspicuous black stripe from bill through eye, otherwise face and chin light buff.
- speculum glossy green with inconspicuous white stripe
  only on lower margin.
- feet yellowish-brown.
- bill uniformly dark greyish-blue.

Distribution and Habitat:
- throughout New Zealand more plentiful in north.
- rivers, lakes, ponds, swamps and inter-tidal mudflats.
- feeds on plants or small insects either on land or in
  shallow water.
- in shallow water, dabbling or "up-ending" is typical.

Breeding:
- September to December.
- Nest: dry grass and other vegetation, lined with down,
  generally away from water, well hidden under cover,
  on the ground, but occasionally in hollow trees or
  tree forks.
- Eggs: 5-11, greenish-cream.
- female only incubates and cares for young.

Note:
Extensive interbreeding with the Mallard has produced
hybrids which may show characteristics of both species.

PLATE 8

27

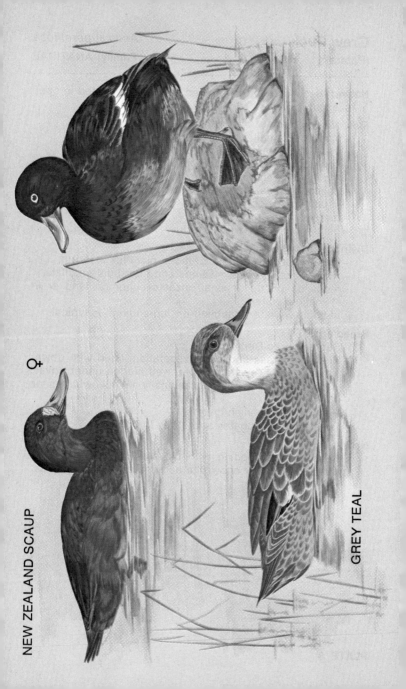

NEW ZEALAND SCAUP

♀

GREY TEAL

New Zealand Scaup
(Papango)

Aythya novaeseelandiae
Family: ANATIDAE

Endemic: (Fully protected)

Field Characters:
- all dark, plump, small duck.
- Male: striking yellow eye and dark head.
- Female: white face patch in breeding plumage, dark eye.
- conspicuous white wing bar on both sexes in flight.
- dives deep for food.

Distribution and Habitat:
- localised throughout both islands on freshwater lakes and ponds.

Breeding:
- October to March.
- Nest: of grass lined with down, close to water, in dense cover or under banks. Often in close groups.
- Eggs: 5-8, creamy-white.

Grey Teal
(Tete)

Anas gibberifrons
Family: ANATIDAE

Native: Also Australia. (Fully protected)

Field Characters:
- much smaller than Grey Duck, but often mistakenly shot as such. Sexes alike.
- rapid wing beat, often seen in wheeling flocks.
- speculum greenish-black, with broad white bar on upper and narrow white bar on lower margin.
- in flight a prominent white triangle shows on underwing with its base close to body.

Distribution and Habitat:
- throughout both islands, more plentiful since 1950s.
- lakes, ponds, lagoons.
- feeds by dabbling, on water insects, snails and plants.

Breeding:
- September to January.
- Nest: of grass, generally lined with down, under vegetation, near water, or in trees.
- Eggs: 5-9, dark-cream.

PLATE 9

NEW ZEALAND SHOVELER

♂

♀

New Zealand Shoveler

(Kuruwhengi)

Anas rhynchotis

Family: ANATIDAE

Endemic: Closely related race in Australia. (Protected, but may be hunted in open season)

Field Characters:
- smaller than Mallard.
- prominent wide bill pointed downwards when swimming.
- Male: "breeding plumage", striking white facial crescent, prominent white patch on flank (lightness of upper breast is variable). "Eclipse plumage" similar to female.
- Female: colouring like female Mallard but with striking powder-blue patch on upper wing.

Distribution and Habitat:
- throughout New Zealand, plentiful in some areas.
- lakes, lagoons, mainly near coast.
- feeds by dabbling.

Breeding:
- October to January.
- Nest: near water (often along ditches), generally of grasses lined with down, among long grass in open areas.
- Eggs: 10-13, pale creamy-white.
- female only incubates, but male assists in rearing young.

PLATE 10

31

AUSTRALASIAN HARRIER

Immature

Adult

Australasian Harrier
(Kahu)

Circus approximans
Family: ACCIPITRIDAE

Native: Also in Australia and S.W. Pacific (Not protected)

Field Characters:
- large bird of prey.
- adults, in contrast to chocolate-brown immature birds, have light buff undersides, with dark streaking.
- some old males appear almost white, with silvery-grey wings.
- in flight, often soars with wings tipped upwards giving broad "vee" image.

Distribution and Habitat:
- fairly common throughout New Zealand except in heavily-forested districts and alpine areas.
- diminishing in numbers by removal of the rabbit and through persecution.
- generally seen singly or in pairs, out of breeding season occasionally flocking at night roosts in swamps.
- feeds mainly on small mammals, insects, lizards, carrion and occasionally small birds, often seen eating road killed animals.

Breeding:
- October to December.
- Nest: platform of tussock and small sticks on ground, mostly in swamps and scrub areas.
- Eggs, commonly 4, chalky-white.

PLATE 11   33

CALIFORNIAN QUAIL

Californian Quail

Lophortyx californicus

Family: PHASIANIDAE

Introduced: From USA 1862. (Protected, but may be hunted in open season in some localities)

Field Characters:
- black crest larger in male than female.
- male's black face surrounded by white band.
- when disturbed rises with a loud "whirring".
- often perches on trees and fence posts.

Distribution and Habitat:
- throughout New Zealand, plentiful in some areas (e.g., Taupo, Marlborough, Central Otago).
- generally farmland with hedges and scrub, occasionally in gardens.
- outside breeding season, mainly in coveys or family groups.
- feeds mainly on seeds and soft grasses.

Breeding:
- October to December.
- simple grass nest in ground hollow near or under cover.
- Eggs: 9-16, creamy-yellow blotched all over with dark brown.
- females only incubate.

Brown Quail

Synoicus ypsilophorus

NOTE:
Introduced from Australia, confined to North Island and numerous in Auckland district. Smaller than Californian, all brown, no crest.

PLATE 12

35

PHEASANT

♀

♂

Pheasant

Phasianus colchicus
Family: PHASIANIDAE

Introduced: Of mixed origins since 1842. Wild stock still supplemented by annual liberations. (Protected but may be hunted in open season)

Field Characters:
- Male: colourful, but varied through hybridisation, some having white neck ring.
- long barred tail.
- Female: drab and slightly smaller.

Distribution and Habitat:
- patchy wild distribution mainly in North Island.
- scrublands and hedgerows.
- feeds on berries, seeds and insects.

Breeding:
- September to January.
- Nest: scantily-lined hollow in thick cover.
- Eggs: 6-14, uniform olive-brown.
- female only incubates and cares for young.
- one cock often breeds with more than one female.

PLATE 13

37

Banded Rail
(Moho-pereru)

Rallus phillippensis
Family: RALLIDAE

Native: Also S.E. Asia, Australia and S.W. Pacific. (Fully protected)

Field Characters:
- black and white striped pattern on underside.
- pronounced chestnut eye streak forming collar at the back of head.
- runs swiftly, rarely seen flying.
- very secretive.

Distribution and Habitat:
- throughout New Zealand, although common, is rarely seen.
- swamps, salt marsh lagoons, lake edges, mangroves, drainage ditches with cover.
- feeds on insects, worms, snails, seeds.

Breeding:
- September to February.
- Nest: of grasses or rushes, well hidden near or above water.
- Eggs: 4-7, pale pinkish-buff with scattered reddish-brown and purplish-grey spots and blotches.

PLATE 14

39

PUKEKO

Pukeko

Porphyrio porphyrio
Family: RALLIDAE

Native: Also in Australia. (Protected, but may be hunted in open season some areas)

Field Characters:
- bright blue and black.
- red bill, frontal shield and legs.
- often flicks tail to show prominent white under tail coverts.
- runs fast, is a reluctant flier, flying heavily with dangling legs.

Distribution and Habitat:
- throughout New Zealand.
- marshes, swamps, lagoons, lakes, riverbanks, with raupo and scrub cover.
- often seen in open near wetlands.
- feeds on wide variety of plant matter, snails, insects, sometimes eggs of other ground-nesting birds.

Breeding:
- August to March.
- Nest: bulky structure in swamp vegetation.
- Eggs: 4-8 normally reddish-cream with variable red-brown spots and purple blotches all over.

PLATE 15   41

AUSTRALIAN COOT

Australian Coot

Fulica atra
Family: RALLIDAE

Native: Straggling from Australia since 1875, large increase and subsequent breeding in 1950s. (Fully protected)

Field Characters:
- slightly smaller than Pukeko.
- mainly seen on water.
- all black with contrasting white bill and frontal shield.
- jerking head when swimming, dives frequently for food.
- Immature: grey with dark bill.

Distribution and Habitat:
- scattered pockets throughout both islands and increasing.
- breeding Otago, Canterbury, Wairarapa, Wanganui, Hawke's Bay and Rotorua.
- frequents reed-fringed lakes.
- feeds on water plants, snails and insects.

Breeding:
- October to December.
- Nest: large and well hidden in swamp vegetation, of sticks and dead rushes according to habitat and neatly lined with raupo leaves.
- Eggs: 5-7, brownish-cream minutely dotted with black spots all over.

PLATE 16   43

SPUR-WINGED PLOVER

Spur-winged Plover

Lobibyx novaehollandiae
Family: CHARADRIIDAE

Native: Straggling from Australia since 1886 and breeding since 1940s. (Fully protected)

Field Characters:
- pigeon size.
- sexes the same.
- slow flapping wing beat.
- crown and shoulders black, back brown, white below.
- distinctive yellow facial wattles.

Distribution and habitat:
- common in Southland and Otago spreading north and straggling to North Island.
- pasture and low crops, often near swamps, water courses and on seashore.
- flocks in autumn.
- feeds on worms and insects.

Breeding:
- July to December.
- Nest: a scrape in ground with virtually no nest material.
- Eggs: 3-4, muddy-green with variable blotching of purplish-brown all over.

PLATE 17

45

ROCK PIGEON

Rock Pigeon

Columba livia
Family: COLUMBIDAE

Introduced: As domesticated races and now wild.
(Not protected)

Field Characters:
- because of the number of original breeds, a widely variable range of plumages from white to black is seen.
- in wild flocks many now reverting to original plumage characters shown in the plate.

Distribution and Habitat:
- throughout New Zealand especially along east coast and in major towns and cities.
- also cliffs, clay banks, seashore and riverbeds.
- feeds mainly on seeds.

Breeding:
- throughout the year.
- Nest: fllmsy, of light sticks, on buildings and ledges, and in cliff crannies.
- Eggs: generally 2, pure white.

PLATE 18   47

LITTLE OWL

Little Owl

Athene noctua

Family: STRIGIDAE

Introduced: Originally from Germany to Otago, 1906. (Partially protected)

Field Characters:
- smaller and lighter in colour than Morepork.
- only owl seen flying and hunting in daylight.
- dipping flight.
- rounded head and wings.

Distribution and Habitat:
- South Island except for mountain ranges, sightings in North Island not confirmed.
- open country and forest edges.
- often seen sitting on fence posts.
- feeds mainly on mice, insects and earthworms, occasionally small birds and lizards.

Breeding:
- September to December.
- Nest: in hollow trees, holes in banks or buildings and occasionally in deserted rabbit burrows. No nest material.
- Eggs: 2-5, round and pure white.

PLATE 19

49

KINGFISHER

Kingfisher

(Kotare)

Halcyon sancta

Family: ALCEDINIDAE

Native: Also Australia. (Fully protected)

Field Characters:
- bright greenish-blue above and off-white to buff below.
- large black pointed bill.
- very short legs.
- direct flight.
- Immature birds: duller in colour with darker mottled breast.

Distribution and Habitat:
- common throughout New Zealand especially in the north.
- wide range of habitat including seashore, open country, bush edges, entering bush along water courses.
- can often be seen perching on power and telephone lines as vantage point.
- feeds by swooping on prey from high perch, mainly mice, lizards, insects, crabs, worms and occasionally dives for small fish.

Breeding:
- October to January.
- Nest: in holes in trees and clay banks dug by the birds. No nest material.
- Eggs: 4-5, shining pure white.

PLATE 20

51

NEW ZEALAND PIPIT

SKYLARK

Skylark

Alauda arvensis
Family: ALAUDIDAE

Introduced: From Europe, 1864 onwards (Not protected)

Field Characters:
- marked crest often raised when startled.
- can be confused with New Zealand Pipit, but has long trilling song mainly while flying.
- rapid wing beats while ascending in a spiral to considerable heights and then slowly descending.
- noticeably longer and straighter hind claw than Pipit.

Distribution and Habitat:
- plentiful throughout New Zealand.
- all types of open country up to high altitude but not alpine.
- feeds mainly on seeds and insects.

Breeding:
- October to January, more than one brood.
- Nest: in ground hollows, a neat grass lined cup well concealed in taller grasses and rushes.
- Eggs: 3-7, yellowish-cream thickly blotched all over with brown and grey, often forming circle at larger end.

New Zealand Pipit
(Pihoihoi)

Anthus novaeseelandiae
Family: MOTACILLIDAE

Native: Very similar species throughout world.
(Fully protected)

Field Characters:
- similar to Skylark, without crest and greyer in colour, light eye stripe more prominent, often flicks tail.
- 'pi-pit' call commonly from low perch.

Distribution and Habitat:
- throughout New Zealand in open or scrub country up to alpine. Often at roadside and on beaches.
- feeds mainly on insects, worms, rarely seeds.

Breeding:
- August to March, more than one brood.
- Nest: on ground, substantial deep cup lined with dry grass, well concealed under vegetation.
- Eggs: 3-4, cream, heavy blotches of brown and grey often concealing cream.

PLATE 21

Welcome Swallow

Hirundo tahitica
Family: HIRUNDINIDAE

Native: S.W. Pacific and Australia, self-introduced, rare straggler prior to 1950s, rapidly spreading.
(Fully protected)

Field Characters:
- smaller than House Sparrow.
- glossy bluish-black with chestnut face and throat.
- strongly forked tail.
- swift erratic flight.

Distribution and Habitat:
- throughout both islands, much more plentiful in North.
- open country close to water, breeding mainly under bridges.
- often seen perching on wires and bare branches.
- gathers in flocks near water in autumn and winter.
- feeds on small flying insects, often above open water.

Breeding:
- September to February, more than one brood.
- Nest: composed of mud pellets reinforced with grass, a shallow cup lined with feathers, mainly under bridges.
- Eggs: 3-5, white, freckled with chestnut spots.

PLATE 22

55

Hedge Sparrow

Prunella modularis
Family: PRUNELLIDAE

Introduced: Originally 1868 from Europe (Not protected)

Field Characters:
- inconspicuous and seemingly solitary.
- similar in size to House Sparrow, but slimmer.
- blue-grey on breast, streaked brown on back, sexes similar.
- moves in short hops with body inclined forward, and flicking movements of wings and raised tail.
- never high above ground except male on song perch.
- short straight flight.

Distribution and Habitat:
- common throughout New Zealand.
- mainly gardens, hedges, scrubland, forest edges and clearings.
- feeds on insects and small seeds.

Breeding:
- August to January.
- Nest: very close to ground in thick cover, neatly lined with mosses, fine grass, hair, occasionally wool.
- Eggs, 3-5, pure intensive turquoise-blue.

PLATE 23

57

FERNBIRD

Fernbird

(Matata)

Bowdleria punctata

Family: MUSCICAPIDAE

Endemic: Six sub-species. (Fully protected)

Field Characters:
- very inconspicuous, mostly in pairs.
- reluctant and poor flier.
- flies with markedly drooping tail.
- untidy tail.
- distinctive sharp metallic call "plik-plik" made by pairs calling to each other.

Distribution and Habitat:
- throughout New Zealand, but becoming localised through loss of habitat.
- swamps, wetlands, bracken and scrublands, not alpine.
- feeds on insects.

Breeding:
- September to February.
- Nest: neatly woven of rushes and grasses, a deep cup lined with feathers, well concealed a few inches from ground or above stagnant water.
- Eggs: 2-3, pinkish-white, with brown dots all over and concentrated near larger end.

PLATE 24

59

Grey Warbler

(Riroriro)

Gerygone igata

Family: MUSCICAPIDAE

Endemic: Closely related species in the Chatham Islands. (Fully protected)

Field Characters:
- smaller than Silvereye.
- conspicuous white tip to tail in flight.
- more commonly heard than seen.
- song, a penetrating high melodious rising and falling trill.
- very active, always on move from perch to perch, often hovers near outside foliage when in search of food.

Distribution and Habitat:
- common throughout New Zealand.
- absent from open country and alpine areas.
- feeds mainly on spiders, insects and their larvae.

Breeding:
- August to December, usually two clutches.
- Nest: hanging pear-shaped structure with side entrance; constructed of grasses, moss, and spiders' web, well lined with feathers.
- Eggs: 3-5, pinkish-white, dotted all over with brown.

Note:
Favourite host of Shining Cuckoo, who lays its egg with second clutch and leaves the warbler to incubate the egg and rear the chick.

PLATE 25

61

FANTAIL

"North Island"

"Black" phase

Fantail

(Piwakawaka)

Rhipidura fuliginosa

Family: MUSCICAPIDAE

Native: Also Australia and the Pacific, with three closely related sub-species in New Zealand. (Fully protected)

Field Characters:
- smaller than House Sparrow.
- chubby body, long tail often fanned.
- erratic butterfly-like flight.
- two colour phases, the "black" phase rare in North Island.
- white ear patch in "black" phase not always present.

Distribution and Habitat:
- throughout New Zealand.
- common in any habitat with trees and shrubs.
- often in small flocks or family groups.
- feeds on insects, especially by "hawking".

Breeding:
- August to January, more than one brood.
- Nest: small firm cup of fibres, moss, bark and hair, coated with spiders' web, with neat fine fibre lining. Often has loose material hanging from base forming a "beard".
- 6-20 feet from ground, usually on a slender branch or horizontal fork, often above water.
- Eggs: 3-4, white with grey and brown spots more dense at larger end.

PLATE 26 63

SONG THRUSH

Song Thrush

Turdus philomelos
Family: MUSCICAPIDAE

Introduced: From Europe 1860s. (Not protected)

Field Characters:
- sexes similar.
- uniform olive-brown above, undersides light buff with bold dark brown spots on breast and flank.
- belly white.
- loud and rapid alarm call "tchik-tchik".

Distribution and Habitat:
- fairly common throughout New Zealand.
- not inside heavy bush, or alpine.
- feeds mostly on ground, snails, worms, insects, also berries and small fruit.

Breeding:
- June to January, more than one clutch.
- Nest: generally low and often conspicuous, big nest of twigs, roots, grasses and mud, the deep cup smoothly lined with wood pulp (mixture of rotten wood and saliva).
- Eggs: 3-5, clear blue with scattered black spots chiefly at larger end.

PLATE 27

65

BLACKBIRD ♂

♀

Blackbird

Turdus merula

Family: MUSCICAPIDAE

Introduced: From Europe 1860s. (Not protected)

Field Characters:
- Male: glossy black with bright yellow bill.
- Female: uniform dark brown above, lighter below with inconspicuous streaks on throat, lightly spotted breast, grey chin, bill generally brown.
- Immature: dark brown with buff streaking on back and rusty brown undersides with dark streaks and speckles.
- partial or total albinos occur.
- voice mellower than song thrush and alarm call a persistent "tchink tchink".

Distribution and Habitat:
- very common throughout New Zealand.
- all habitats except alpine.
- feeds mainly on ground, worms and often fruit.

Breeding:
- July to January, more than one clutch.
- Nest: often conspicuous on trees, shrubs, hedges, and frequently on or in buildings; big and often untidy of grasses, roots and fibres bound with mud. Deep cup lined with grass and rootlets.
- Eggs: 2-4, dull turquoise, thickly freckled with red-brown.

PLATE 28

67

SILVEREYE

Silvereye
(Tauhou)

Zosterops lateralis
Family: ZOSTEROPIDAE

Native: Also S.E. Australia, self-introduced mid-1800s.
  (Partially protected)

Field Characters:
  - smaller than House Sparrow.
  - distinctive white eye ring.
  - bright yellowish-green above with grey saddle, light grey breast and rusty flanks.
  - most obvious in winter when moving in flocks.

Distribution and Habitat:
  - throughout New Zealand.
  - all areas with tree cover including subalpine scrub, not obvious except in flocks.
  - feeds on insects, nectar, berries and fruit.

Breeding:
  - August to February, more than one clutch.
  - Nest: very fllmsy structure of fine grasses and fibres attached like a hammock with spiders' web to twigs or leaves in outermost foliage.
  - Eggs: 3-4, clear pale blue, can often be seen through walls of nest.

PLATE 29

69

CIRL
BUNTING

♂

♀

YELLOWHAMMER

♂

Yellowhammer

Emberiza citrinella
Family: EMBERIZIDAE

Introduced: From Europe 1860s. (Not protected)

Field Characters:
- similar in size to House Sparrow.
- Male: bright yellow head and undersides with dark chest band. Female: more drab.
- both sexes have conspicuous chestnut rump, and mainly white outer tail feathers which are prominent in flight.
- large flocks in winter and spring.

Distribution and Habitat:
- throughout New Zealand, mainly in open country to alpine tussock.
- feeds on seeds and insects.

Breeding:
- October to January.
- Nest: generally close to ground in scrub, hedges, fern, gorse, etc., of grasses lined with finer grass and hair.
- Eggs: 3-5, variable pink to purplish-white, erratically patterned with finely pencilled dark lines.

Cirl Bunting

Emberiza cirlus
Family: EMBERIZIDAE

Introduced: From Europe 1870s. (Not protected)

Field Characters:
- similar to Yellowhammer.
- Male: adult has prominent black throat and eyestripe, olive-green rump.
- Female: no chestnut rump otherwise similar to female Yellowhammer.

Distribution and Habitat:
- mainly east coast of South Island, rare in North Island. Habitat similar to Yellowhammer.

Breeding:
- similar to Yellowhammer, but eggs less prominently marked.

PLATE 30   71

CHAFFINCH ♂

♀

Chaffinch

Fringilla coelebs
Family: FRINGILLIDAE

Introduced: From Europe, 1860s. (Not protected)

Field Characters:
- Male colourful. Female drab. Immature similar to adult female.
- Male and female, have two conspicuous white bars on wing and white outer tail feathers prominent in flight.
- flight undulating.

Distribution and Habitat:
- throughout New Zealand, nowhere in large numbers.
- mainly gardens, orchards and scrubland, but also throughout exotic forest and native bush up to the scrubline.
- outside the breeding season often in loose flocks of separate sexes.
- during winter, single birds often seen mixed in flocks of other finches.
- feeds on insects, and seeds.

Breeding:
- October to February.
- Nest: neat and tightly woven of moss, grass and fine roots. Always plastered on the outside with moss and lichen, lined with fine grass, thistledown and feathers. Often built close to tree trunk, at fork of branch.
- Eggs: 4-6 **either** purplish and red-brown splodges on a grey to green-blue background **or** pure blue with slight black-purplish spots.

PLATE 31   73

GREENFINCH

♂

♀

Greenfinch

Carduelis chloris

Family: FRINGILLIDAE

Introduced: From Europe 1860s. (Not protected)

Field Characters:
- larger than House Sparrow.
- forked tail, heavy pale bill.
- Male: olive-green, with bright yellow markings on wings and tail very striking in flight.
- Female and Immature: duller and browner.

Distribution and Habitat:
- quite plentiful throughout New Zealand up to 2000ft.
- open country, gardens, hedges and pine plantations.
- flocks in autumn.
- feeds on seeds, fleshy fruits, insect larvae, occasionally leaves and fruit flowers.

Breeding:
- September to January, usually two broods.
- Nest: often in fork rarely higher than 20ft., of fine sticks, roots and moss, lined with feathers, wool and hair.
- Eggs: 4-6, off-white with variable red-brown spots or streaks.

PLATE 32

75

GOLDFINCH

Adult

Immature

Goldfinch

Carduelis carduelis
Family: FRINGILLIDAE

Introduced: From Europe 1860s. (Not protected)

Field Characters:
- smaller than House Sparrow.
- sexes alike.
- distinctive red, white and black head.
- conspicuous broad yellow band on black wings.
- Immature: streaky light brown underside and lacks bright head colours.
- often in flocks.

Distribution and Habitat:
- throughout New Zealand.
- common in settled areas, especially abundant in fruit-growing areas.
- rare above 3000ft.
- feeds mainly on seed heads, especially composites (dandelion, thistle, etc.) and grasses, insects and their larvae.

Breeding:
- September to December, usually two broods.
- Nest: neat round structure of grass roots, cobwebs, hair, lined either with thistledown, wool or feathers.
- 5-12ft. from ground in trees and shrubs, often in outside branches.
- Eggs: 4-6, bluish-white, with reddish spots and blotches especially at larger end.

PLATE 33   77

REDPOLL   ♀

♂

Redpoll

Acanthis flammea
Family: FRINGILLIDAE

Introduced: From Europe 1860s. (Not protected)

Field Characters:
- smaller than House Sparrow and smallest of introduced finches.
- superficially drab.
- crimson forehead and small black bib.
- the male breast has a variable amount of pink which can sometimes be absent.
- Immature: crimson on forehead absent.

Distribution and Habitat:
- common throughout New Zealand.
- especially in scrubland, generally away from towns, but up to subalpine.
- feeds mainly on seeds, insects and soft parts of plants.

Breeding:
- September to January, often two broods.
- Nest: mainly in shrubs, small and compact of grass, twigs and wool, lined with hair, feathers or wool.
- Eggs: 4-5, bluish-white with dark or light brown spots and streaks.

PLATE 34

79

HOUSE SPARROW

♂

Summer

Autumn

♂

♀

House Sparrow

Passer domesticus
Family: PLOCEIDAE

Introduced: From Europe 1860s. (Not protected)

Field Characters:
- most commonly seen bird in built-up areas.
- Males: black bib varying in size, small in autumn, large in summer because of wear of feathers exposing their black bases. Bill black in breeding season, otherwise brown.
- Immature and female: similarly drab.

Distribution and Habitat:
- abundant throughout New Zealand.
- prefers areas close to habitation, less plentiful on open grassland, not penetrating far into forest.
- often in flocks. Large night roosts common in cities.
- feeds widely on insects, seeds, scraps, grain, fruits, flax nectar, according to locality and season.

Breeding:
- July to April, several broods.
- Nest: usually in holes in buildings, trees and cliffs, also colonies in high trees where nests are large untidy-looking structures of grass with side entrances, and lined with feathers.
- Eggs: 5-7, white, generally heavily spotted and streaked with greyish-brown.

PLATE 35 81

STARLING   Adult Winter

Immature

Summer

♂

Starling

Sturnus vulgaris
Family: STURNIDAE

Introduced: From Europe 1862. (Not protected)

Field Characters:
- slightly smaller than Blackbird.
- short tail, pointed wings prominent in flight.
- winter plumage: sexes similar, blackish speckled with buff, bill black.
- breeding plumage: bill yellow, males black with purple and green gloss, females retain much of buff speckling.
- Immature: dull brownish buff with dark bill.
- form extensive and noisy roosting flocks outside breeding season.

Distribution and Habitat:
- very common throughout New Zealand, up to subalpine, except in dense bush.
- feeds on worms, insects, fruit, often on open paddocks and beaches.

Breeding:
- September to January, often two broods.
- Nest: in holes in buildings, trees, cliffs and banks, an untidy accumulation of straw and grasses.
- Eggs: 4-6, plain pale blue, with slight gloss.

PLATE 36   83

INDIAN MYNA

Indian Myna

Acridotheres tristis
Family: STURNIDAE

Introduced: Initially from Australia 1870s. (Not protected)

Field Characters:
- similar in size to Blackbird.
- bright yellow bill, legs and bare patch below eye.
- conspicuous white patch on wing and tip of tail in flight.
- Immature: grey-brown head.
- often form communal night roosts outside breeding season.

Distribution and Habitat:
- plentiful in North Island northwards from Wanganui and Southern Hawke's Bay, occasionally south of this line.
- characteristically in built-up areas, often seen at roadside.
- feeds mainly on insects, some fruit and seeds.

Breeding:
- November to February, generally two broods.
- Nest: an untidy accumulation of grasses, plastics, cellulose and green leaves, in holes in buildings, trees and banks.
- Eggs: 3-5, pale blue.

PLATE 37

85

BLACK-BACKED
MAGPIE

♀

♂

Black-backed Magpie *Gymnorhina tibicen tibicen*

Family: CRACTICIDAE

Introduced: Details unknown. (Not protected)

Field Characters:
- conspicuous black and white bird.
- black back distinguishes this sub-species from White-backed Magpie.
- hindneck white in male but mottled grey in female.
- Immature: mottled grey underside and back, with grey hindneck.
- melodious flute-like call.

Distribution and Habitat:
- restricted to Hawke's Bay and Turakina districts of North Island, Cheviot and Kaikoura in South Island.
- hybridises with White-backed Magpie producing mixed progeny with varying amounts of black on the back. These may be seen over wide areas.
- food as for White-backed Magpie.

Breeding:
- see White-backed Magpie.

PLATE 38

87

WHITE-BACKED MAGPIE

♀

♂

White-backed Magpie

Gymnorhina tibicen hypoleuca
Family: CRACTICIDAE

Introduced: From Australia 1860s. (Not protected)

Field Characters:
- similar to Black-backed Magpie.
- Male: back white.
- Female: back grey.
- Immature: similar to female but with mottled grey underside.
- melodious flute-like call.

Distribution and Habitat:
- throughout New Zealand.
- except thick bush and alpine areas, commonly on outskirts of built-up areas including parks, golf courses, etc.
- feeds generally on insects, worms, occasionally eggs and young of ground-nesting birds.

Breeding:
- August to November, occasionally two broods.
- Nest: usually in tall trees, an untidy collection of twigs, wire and other sundries often used, lined with roots and fibres.
- Eggs: 2-5, bluish-green, heavily blotched all over with greyish-brown.

Note:
Boldly defends its nesting territory by dive-bombing intruders, including human beings who approach the area too closely.

PLATE 39

89

ROOK

Adult

Immature

Rook

Corvus frugilegus
Family: CORVIDAE

Introduced: From Europe 1860s. (Not protected)

Field Characters:
- bigger than Magpie.
- all black with bluish gloss and large black bill, sexes alike.
- only adults have bare grey skin surrounding base of bill.
- deliberate wing beat.
- large flocks form regular night roosts outside breeding season.

Distribution and Habitat:
- mainly Hawke's Bay, South Wairarapa and Canterbury, with largest concentration in Hawke's Bay. Occasional elsewhere.
- open country and plantations.
- feeds on insects, worms, larvae, seeds and vegetable matter.

Breeding:
- September to October.
- Nest: in tops of large trees, large and untidy of twigs and mud with grass lining, used from year to year.
- generally close together forming "rookeries" which may be very large.
- Eggs: 2-4, pale bluish-green closely covered with greyish-brown blotches and spots.

PLATE 40   91

Index of Common Names

Volume 1—Town, Pasture and Freshwater
Volume 2—Mountain, Bush and Shore

Mallard	1	7
Morepork	2	31
Myna	1	37
Owl, Little	1	19
Oystercatcher, South Island Pied	2	14
Oystercatcher, Variable	2	14
Parakeet, Red-crowned	2	29
Parakeet, Yellow-crowned	2	29
Penguin, Blue	2	3
Penguin, Fiordland Crested	2	2
Penguin, White-flippered	2	3
Penguin, Yellow-eyed	2	2
Pheasant	1	13
Pigeon, New Zealand	2	26
Pigeon, Rock	1	18
Pipit	1	21
Plover, Spur-winged	1	17
Pukeko	1	15
Quail, Californian	1	12
Rail, Banded	1	14
Redpoll	1	34
Rifleman	2	32
Robin	2	38
Rook	1	40
Rosella, Eastern	2	28
Scaup	1	9
Shag, Black	2	5
Shag, Little	2	6
Shag, Little Black	2	6
Shag, Pied	2	5
Shag, Spotted	2	8
Shag, Stewart Island	2	7
Shoveler	1	10
Silvereye	1	29
Skylark	1	21
Sparrow, Hedge	1	23
Sparrow, House	1	35
Spoonbill, Royal	2	9
Starling	1	36
Stilt, Pied	2	19
Swallow, Welcome	1	22

Swan, Black	1	4
Teal, Grey	1	9
Tern, Black-fronted	2	23
Tern, Caspian	2	24
Tern, White-fronted	2	25
Thrush, Song	1	27
Tit	2	37
Tui	2	40
Warbler, Grey	1	25
Weka	2	13
Whitehead	2	35
Wren, Rock	2	33
Wrybill	2	17
Yellowhead	2	36
Yellowhammer	1	30

ACKNOWLEDGEMENTS

The artist and the authors wish to acknowledge the assistance and advice of G. Marshall, the National Museum and the staff of the Wildlife Branch, Department of Internal Affairs.

The Mobil New Zealand Nature Series

New Zealand Native Trees II

Nancy M. Adams

The long-awaited sequel to **New Zealand Native Trees I,** this volume, beautifully illustrated by the author, identifies and describes some thirty-two species of native tree found throughout New Zealand from mountain rain forest to lowland bush and scrub.

Common Ferns in New Zealand

R. J. Chinnock and Eric Heath

New Zealand is renowned the world over for the abundance and variety of its fern life. Here some sixty species of fern, some of them unique to this country, are presented in full colour, with informative notes on life history, cultivation, classification and identification.

Seashore Life in New Zealand

R. K. Dell and Eric Heath

A useful introduction to the main groups of sea life found on our shores, from shellfish to seaweeds, sea slugs to octopi. This colourful and meticulously researched volume will be a delight to beachcomber and student alike.

Marine Fishes in New Zealand

J. M. Moreland and Eric Heath

This volume describes and illustrates in colour a wide variety of the sea-fish likely to be taken in New Zealand waters. With each illustration goes the species' common, Maori and scientific names, a list of habitats and salient characteristics, diet and method of catching. An angler's and cook's delight!

Mushrooms and Toadstools in New Zealand

Marie Taylor

Marie Taylor's combined talents as biologist and illustrator are here brought together in this survey of some of the wide variety of mushrooms and fungi found in New Zealand's fields and woods. They range from the deadly poisonous to the eminently edible, but all are a feast for the eye, and all exemplify the extraordinary diversity of this country's rich flora.

Common Insects in New Zealand I and II

Annette Walker and Eric Heath

These two volumes each cover some thirty-two species of insect found around the home and in the garden, in the bush and near the shore. Accompanying each page of text are a series of beautiful and highly authoritative drawings showing the development and life cycle of the individual species, many of which are seldom recognised and little understood.

Uncommon Birds in New Zealand

Janet Marshall, F. C. Kinsky, C. J. R. Robertson

Forty rarely-seen birds illustrated in full colour, accompanied by a descriptive text by two of New Zealand's leading ornithologists. Many of the species are seldom seen even by professional ornithologists, and some are considered extinct.